CW00640997

VISIONS

by

Julien Chilcott-Monk

Julien Chilcott-Monk lives with his wife in Winchester. His principal interests are music and the written word. His writing has taken him from ghosts to a dramatic adaptation of Evelyn Waugh's 'Edmund Campion' and to early music. This is his first devotional work. His second, 'The Gospel of Tom the Shepherd', is nearing completion as finishing touches are added to his new edition of the thirteenth century liturgical drama 'The Play of Daniel'.

Tufton Books
Faith House
7 Tufton Street
London SW1P 4QN

Distributed by Gracewing

First published in Great Britain 1996

© Tufton Books (Church Union Publication) 1997

ISBN 0 -85244-400-1

All rights reserved; no part of this publication may be reproduced, stored in a retrieval system, or transmitted in any form or by any means, electronic, mechanical, photocopying, recording, or otherwise without either the prior written permission of the Publishers or a licence permitting restricted copying in the United Kingdom issued by the Copyright Licensing Agency Ltd, 90 Tottenham Court Road, London W1P 9HE. This book may not be lent, resold, hired out or otherwise disposed of by way of trade in any form of binding or cover other than that in which it is published, without the prior consent of the Publishers.

1 3 5 7 9 10 8 6 4 2

Typeset by Phoenix Photosetting, Chatham, Kent
Printed and bound in Great Britain by
Ashford Colour Press, Gosport, Hampshire

Contents

For my Godchildren Julien, Alexander, Nicholas, Paul, Susanna and Andrew.

May their own visions lead them to a closer understanding of the Christian Faith.

Preface

by The Bishop of London

One of the great spiritual figures of the Christian East, Isaac of Nineveh, taught that Scripture is an ocean that will never finish being explored. Those growing in Christ need to dive into the depths of meaning by careful study and attentive prayer. It is superficial to swim around on the surface.

I am sure that many will be grateful to Mr Chilcott-Monk for his imaginative exploration of the Gospel stories. It is obvious to readers of these meditations that they come out of a prayerful encounter and that at the centre of them lies an invitation to us to engage with the story of Jesus Christ not merely with our critical faculties, but with what the Fathers describe as 'the mind in the heart'.

+Richard Londin:

Introduction

These stories were conceived to be read aloud at six successive annual services of nine lessons and carols. Although they may again be so used, they are presented here primarily as aids to private contemplation and devotion. Even so, the Bible readings suggested in the appendix for use at carol services in conjunction with these stories, may well be of help to the private reader of this book.

The characters and their visions spring from the imagination prompted only by a name or oblique reference in one of the Gospels or a non-canonical work. The hope is that the reader of 'Visions' will be encouraged to return to the Prophets of the Old Testament and the Gospels of the New after having been caught up in the enthusiasm and excitement of the characters.

'Visions' should be regarded as nothing more than a few flowers scattered at the base of the column of Truth.

JC-M
St John Vianney
August 1996

The Visions of the Shepherd

Imagine, if you will, three shepherds; we shall suppose, three. So there are three Jewish shepherds, who, huddled together under woollen blankets, keep watch for the wolf. The youngest of the three has a fine crook, a neck crook. The forging is fine, the scroll delicately worked, the shaft smooth and fine-grained. The young man idly looks through the broad arch of the crook to the stars and to the moon. He frames the brightness of the moon within the arch. His mind wanders to what scripture has told him of the creation of the world, the moon, and the stars.

The young man, he is but fifteen or so, continues to gaze and recall the scripture. Was it not Isaiah who said of the Messiah that he should feed his flock like a shepherd? The shepherd-boy feels of importance for a moment. He remembers more of Isaiah's words and how that prophet gave details of the birth of the Messiah. He contemplates the hope with excitement.

Still he gazes moonwards. His uncle, one of the two white-haired companions, taps him on the shoulder and says: 'You won't see the wolf up there, my lad!'

The nephew stands and scours the hillside, but only for a moment or two. His uncle returns to the embrace of slumber as our young man allows his eyes to be drawn again to the moon through the arch of his crook. He again recalls the prophecies of old, and allows his mind to drift away from his work.

Our shepherd is filled with the thrill of anticipation. He cannot think why: he has heard the Messianic prophecies in the synagogue many times. They always make him happy. But how shall such a Messiah and Saviour be born into the world? He stares again at the stars and the moon. His eyes fall from the sky to the shaft of the crook. By the moonlight he sees the fine grain of the wood and watches, startled, as the grain coarsens before his eyes. The wood leaves his hand and becomes a rough doorpost. He sees a young woman kneeling before a splendidly-brilliant, white-clad figure: her hand holds fast the doorpost steadying her genuflexion. The young shepherd finds himself standing not four paces from this young woman.

He watches in awe as the woman, in great humility, says: 'Let it be according to your word'. So this is God's marvellous plan. He watches the vision, though round him the sheep are still bleating and his fellows are now snoring.

— ❁ —

The young shepherd blinks his eyes and the vision fades. He wonders if he should wake his companions. He decides not to do so: they would think him stupid. The vision is gone and the crook is back in his hand. But he cannot resist and, after only a short while, looks again through the arch of his crook. Once more, the moonlight fills the iron frame. This time the result is quite different: a more brilliant light fills the frame. It bursts out all around. The older men are awakened by the light. The light is blinding, brighter far than the star that has for some time been shining down upon them, and upon Bethlehem at the foot of the hill.

Having been urged to leave their flock by the very messengers of God, the three shepherds stand at a respectful distance. A mother is nursing her newborn child. Is this the King, the Saviour of the world? Is this the Messiah whom the prophets expected, born in a cattle house? They begin to understand that this is indeed the long-awaited Saviour. They kneel. Our young hero is overcome, because the woman before him is the woman from his vision on the hilltop.

The lamb he has been carrying drops from his shoulders, and scampers to the manger close beside the young woman and child. It settles in the straw.

The stable is large: it smells like a stable, of course, and it is warm enough by comparison with the hillside. But is it the palace of a king?

After a time the shepherds return to the hillside and watch a great procession of torches and camels. Rich, fine foreigners are travelling towards Bethlehem, travelling from far-distant lands. The shepherds hear that these are wise men, who, guided by the meaning of the bright star, are seeking a young male child, born to be a special king.

So the Messiah is being shown to the world – to the Gentiles as well as the Jews – as the prophets foretold.

The shepherds talk excitedly among themselves but our young shepherd stands a little way off. An old sheep lies down beside him, rather in the manner of a pet dog. The young man grips the shaft of his crook firmly and looks again through the loop of it. Shall this small child conquer the world from such humble beginnings? How? He finds that the moon has moved a long way across the sky and is dipping towards the earth. He causes the moon to be framed by his crook. He looks at the shaft: again the grain has coarsened; this time it seems to burst into leaf. He is under a fig tree and from this vantage-point he sees our Lord as a man, gathering the disciples; he hears the Sermon on the Mount, 'Blessed are the pure in heart, for they shall see God'; he sees the feeding of thousands on a hillside, and the healing of many. He sees the trial of Jesus, the fickle crowd having cried, 'Hosanna!' one day, crying, 'Crucify!' the next. And, worst of all, does he see himself in that fickle crowd? Surely that cannot be.

The vision fades; he is momentarily blinded by his own tears. But it is not yet over; he is drawn again to the light, to the vision. The leaves on the wood have died. The shaft seems to reduce in size; it becomes the handle of a leather whip. He witnesses

5

the scourging, the procession with the cross and the horrific crucifixion of Jesus.

Our shepherd is aghast. The crook is back in his hand. His fellows are still chattering happily but he is in deep despair. Fearing the continuation of the vision his eyes are only reluctantly drawn to the top of the crook. The crook once more feels rough to his touch as it is wrenched from him by an unseen force. The shaft is now a huge cross and the shepherd is at the foot of it looking up at the crucified Lord. He backs away. He sees Mary, now much older and full of grief, and some others he does not recognize. Almost immediately, blackness envelops him: there are no stars.

It is morning: he has in his hand the shaft only of his crook. He is walking towards a hillside tomb in the company of others. 'Bring a stake' they have said 'to move the stone so that the womenfolk can place spices on the body.' But the stone has already been moved and the body is gone – risen from the dead. The young man sees Jesus appear before them saying: 'I am the good shepherd: follow me.'

He shakes his head and finds himself still holding the crook and standing with the old sheep at his feet. His companions are still engrossed in conversation. He joins them bemused, and together they look down the hillside upon the stable, and the camels of the elaborate foreigners waiting outside.

Our young shepherd turns away and glances for the last time through the top of his crook: again the brilliant light. Then he sees heaven in its vastness; he sees the crooks and croziers in the hands of future shepherds in the shoes of Christ and his Apostles, and he sees the saints of all ages praising with the angels, God the Father, the Son and the Holy Spirit. He sees Mary enthroned beside Jesus, who, in the glory and majesty of God and the power of the Holy Spirit, presides at the great festival. He sees that the saints are often glamourless work-a-day men and women, good priests and nuns equal with the great and the lowly. He sees Christ's glory reflected in their faces and he knows then how they lived their lives on earth. The heavenly chorus continually sings its prayers for the living and the dead, and for peace to men of good will.

The visions disappear; our shepherd needs them no more, for the story is about to unfold – God's plan in place from the beginning of time.

The Visions of the Wise Men

Tradition has named the wise men of St Matthew's Gospel, and tradition asserts that there were three of them. For the sake of continuity, let us therefore retain the names: Baltazar, Gaspar and Melchior. These men travelled from the East, from well outside the Roman Empire. But why did they make the journey? What was their story?

For many days the man Melchior, an old and highly-respected philosopher, astrologer and astronomer, had searched his books and had taken measurements from his charts of the night-sky with delicate instruments. He had made calculation after calculation until his venerable eyes had grown tired.

His long, sparse white beard curled upwards at the end. His wrinkled oriental face with its golden complexion revealed a kindly nature, and almost complete exhaustion. He must inform the Grand Lord, his master, of his conclusions.

'My Lord,' he said 'I have discovered a star in the heavens, a star ever-brightening.'

'What does it mean, pray?' asked his Lord.

'I believe it to foretell the birth of a king.'

'A king?' cried the War Lord in mock alarm. 'A king to challenge the authority of this throne, by any chance?'

Melchior raised a hand gently. 'No, no, my Lord: a king of a very different kingdom, I believe; but any more I do not understand.'

'You are tired, old man. Go, search for your king and return refreshed. Take what you will for your journey.'

Melchior returned to his studio and bade his servants prepare mules and provisions. He looked again at his calculations. 'Yes, certainly a king,' he said to himself with some satisfaction, and then gazed out of the window at the star. A shaft of light seemed to penetrate his tired eyes, and he saw a messenger of the heavens bathed in the white light of the star, standing before a young woman who, kneeling, was saying to the messenger 'Be it unto me according to thy word'. The tired eyes blinked and the vision was gone.

Great joy overcame this learned man and he reasoned that he would have to travel a great distance towards the west. And, as his mule-train was being prepared, he selected a large golden casket as a gift for the newborn king.

9

Like Melchior, who had by now been travelling for many weeks, Gaspar believed that he had discovered the meaning of the star. He was advanced in the study of the stars. He too had calculated, studied and made searching observations. Gaspar held an important position: he had the confidence of his king. Gaspar was of a dark-skinned people: he was middle-aged with a large family. Much of his time was spent in the service of the king, which Gaspar considered an honour and a privilege. He was immensely happy when he entered the presence of his king.

'Most Honourable Sir! From the revelations of the stars, I predict the birth of a male child of some significance. It is most wonderful news.'

'Wonderful, indeed. Find the boy, by all means, and pay homage on behalf of my kingdom.'

Gaspar had learned the scripture and the prophecies of many of the lands beyond his own – the Babylonian annals, the Persian myths, and, above all, the writings of the Hebrew and Jewish prophets. The evidence pointed to the long-awaited Saviour of the whole world. But what would be the nature of this Saviour?

Already, the king's bearers were making ready all he would need for his westward journey. He would begin that very night. He lingered in his clay-bricked study, and glanced through a glass lens at the star, as he had done countless times. Whereupon a fine reed of light passed through the prism at the edge of his glass, and coloured lights burst about the room. He saw a man, bearded and clad in alb being dipped in a river at another man's hands. As the man rose from the water the baptizer knelt, as though he felt himself unworthy to perform the baptism. The crowd on the bank clapped, and thunder rolled overhead. Gaspar heard distinctly: 'This is my beloved Son.' The reed of light receded, the glass blackened and he saw no more. With excitement, he thought 'This Saviour will be none other than the Son of God'. He looked up to the skies and spread his hands in amazement.

Gaspar prepared for his journey forthwith. He clasped his family one by one and took his leave of them, but the smallest child clung resolutely to his robe, pressing his little brown face to his father's leg. The child's mother gently prized him away with not a little sorrow.

In the saddlebag of his own horse, Gaspar stowed most expensive and precious perfumes, incenses and gums, brought originally from the very lands through which he would soon be travelling - a gift for a God.

And so to Baltazar from the Persian lands. By his sighting of the star, it was revealed to him that a boy would be born to change the course of the history of the world. Baltazar's country's ancient writings had pointed to such an event, and across the sands in the land of Israel the Jews had long held such a belief. He would search for the child in that land. His master and the chiefest of his land approved his journey and wished him well, giving him myrrh and rich spices – a present fit for a mortal of some worth.

Baltazar was a wise and learned man and interpreted the stars, dreams and signs for the greatest. Like Melchior he was lightly bearded and about as ancient, though his white, smooth skin admitted of fewer years.

Camels were prepared, and attendants placed at the wise man's disposal. Food and tents were loaded onto the animals, and musicians and a few warriors made themselves ready. In a moment of self-doubt, Baltazar shaded his eyes and squinted at the star, which began to shine as brilliantly as the sun at midday and flooded a temple courtyard in light. The courtyard was unknown to Baltazar. But there were there some moneychangers deceiving the gullible, the old and the unwise. A man appeared in their midst and in righteous anger overthrew the tables of these deceitful men. Baltazar was impressed by the reaction of the ordinary people, though he noticed a knot of temple officials clearly displeased and conspiring. He heard the man say: 'But you have made it a den of thieves.' The spectacle disappeared: the star shone as before. 'Certainly a man to change the world!' Baltazar said with some emotion and pride.

His camel rose and the train set off slowly. After a few miles, the rearguard announced the sighting of a large band of travellers heading towards them.

— ❁ —

The three wise men meet. Together they follow the star. Melchior and Gaspar are now seated upon camels, and the company is large. As they set up camp for the night, they share food and entertainment, happy in the knowledge that they are firmly resolved to seek after the truth together. And so with interpreters, lively minds and this single aim, the wise men share their insights, visions and conclusions. The picture thus painted confuses them and puzzles them greatly. They have travelled for many weeks; they are sure that they are coming to the land of their visions; they require yet another sign, but their resolve is certain.

They sit together at the camp fire: the star shines, that constant companion of the nights. This night is unusually cold, in fact a little snow lies on the ground. Their fine robes glow in the flickering light of the fire and they fall silent . . . waiting.

Gaspar looks at the star, and a faint trickle of light – like a thin strand of spider's silk – drops on to a far-distant hillside, and is gone. He then sees a brilliance in the sky above that hillside, and messengers of God announcing the birth of him whom they seek. He sees the incredulous looks of some shepherds. The youngest is overawed, and this young man carries an orphaned lamb over his shoulders as they set off down the hillside. And Gaspar sees no more.

'Ah!' exclaims Gaspar suddenly. 'The good God reveals his purpose first to the ordinary, simple folk, and then to all lands, in the persons of three philosophers from Eastern countries. We must aim, eventually, for the region of that distant hill, absolutely.' He announces this in triumph, his voice breaking with excitement.

These sages are now not far from Jerusalem. They are tired, for they have recently crossed the River Jordan. They are within Roman territory, and specifically within the jurisdiction of Herod the Great. Out of courtesy, they resolve to call upon that king before they search further.

Before the travellers begin their journey to Herod's palace in Jerusalem, messengers are sent from the palace to invite the wise men to an audience. Meanwhile, they talk together of their visions. They agree that there is nothing fortuitous about their meeting, or about the visions they have been granted. God is nudging them in the right direction, enabling them to understand something of the miracle and to pay homage on behalf of the whole world. They amaze themselves in their musings. They are almost at their destination, yet they are not certain where precisely the star is leading them. What are they to understand?

For the umpteenth time, Melchior rehearses his vision of a young woman receiving God's commission to bear the child. Gaspar enthusiastically reminds the two older men how he has seen a man – the child they are seeking, as a grown man – acknowledged by God as His Son. They consider carefully and Baltazar says: 'But, in my vision, he was simply a good man much concerned about bad behaviour in the temple precincts.'

'The Son of God zealous for his Father's house,' proposes Gaspar gently.

'A king!' Melchior insists.

Deep in thought they rise and prepare to enter Jerusalem.

Our three learned men return to their camp outside Jerusalem and make ready to travel to the small city of Bethlehem a few miles from Jerusalem.

They have shown their gifts to Herod – the gifts they prepared for the child, in their own countries – and are still expressing surprise at Herod's reaction. He appeared angry; and then in an apparent change of mood asked them to report to him on finding the child.

Baltazar now walks on his own, away from the camp. Night is falling and the star shines brightly. 'What manner of man will this child be?' he asks himself out loud.

He remembers the man who overturned the tables of the moneychangers. He is deep in thought and finds himself being pressed forward by a crowd to see the man heal a dumb man, a leper, and someone who is lame. The crowd surges forward and Baltazar falls to the ground in a pool of light, the vision at an end. A servant rushes to help the old man to his feet. He remembers then something of the words of Isaiah: 'In those days the dumb shall speak, the lepers shall be cleansed and the lame shall walk.'

He remembers that, in the distance, beyond the crowds, the same conspirators were plotting. Is this the Christ, the word of God made flesh, made man?

Will he have to suffer at the hands of the very people he is sent to save?

Baltazar's ancient mind is under a great strain. The child they are about to visit is to be the Light of the Jews and the Light of the Gentiles.

— ❀ —

Melchior rests in his elaborate tent. He finds comforting his colourful clothes, his colourful carpets. He closes his eyes and rests his head, and his mind drifts from Herod's palace to the memorable stations on his long journey; he recalls his home, his studio. The star peeps through his tent flap outside which crackles the fire. Nevertheless, he shivers and seems to sense death – but not his own. The flap opens wide as a result of a freak gust of wind; the star's light floods into the tent as brightly as the sun. He is on the side of a hill looking up towards the top. Then rapidly the sun is eclipsed and he is shrouded in an eerie darkness. He just makes out that upon the hill there are three men crucified. He moves closer. The man upon the cross, in between two others, Melchior recognizes as the man described by Gaspar and Baltazar. But now he is beaten and bruised. Above the head of Christ he sees 'This is the King of the Jews' written in three languages. Why are they killing the king God has sent? Do they not know? Melchior's eyes fall upon the young woman from his vision, now a middle-aged woman grieving for her son, her shoulders bent in anguish, being comforted by another. The crucified Christ commends his spirit to God his father, and dies. Horror grips Melchior's stomach. Suddenly the hillside is empty save for the cross of Christ. Melchior hears the voice heard by Gaspar: 'This is my beloved Son.' There is nothing upon the hillside but the majestic figure of Christ. Transformed is the body racked with pain. He remains upon the cross, but he is now clothed in fine vestments with a golden crown upon his head in place of the cruel thorns.

'Then', says Melchior aloud as he awakes from his vision, 'he shall reign as from the cross. The child-king before whom we shall soon bow down is of a very different kingdom indeed.'

The wise men make their journey to the foot of a hill beside Bethlehem, and from there some shepherds guide them to where the young child rests.

At their new camp to the south of Bethlehem, Melchior explains to his fellows the vision of the gruesome crucifixion as they exchange their precious memories of the serenity and resolution of Mary, the patience and acquiescence of Joseph, and the divine nobility of the little child Jesus.

Baltazar reveals his vision of the healing miracles, his remembrance of Isaiah's words, and his understanding.

Gaspar's brown face is moist with tears as he falteringly concludes: 'Friends, this is the Saviour of the world who will, only by being tortured, broken and killed, redeem mankind. The prophets have been ignored, and God himself shunned. This Saviour is none other than God himself, incarnate for the world; and in this form he too will be rejected.'

'Then how will he redeem the world?' asks Baltazar.

'By engulfing death and sin and the devil, with the sacrifice of his very self.'

They are close together around the fire as night falls; the star is no longer necessary to them for their journeying, but for the last time it brightens and casts around their camp a circle of light. The three men find themselves in a hillside garden not far from a sepulchre hewn out of rock. Outside the tomb a man is standing beside a woman. The woman is in much distress and is staring at the ground. 'They have taken him away and I do not know where they have laid him!' she sobs.

Melchior sees a kingly crown upon the man's head; Baltazar sees the marks of crucifixion on his hands and feet; and Gaspar sees the glory of God shining from him. Together, they hear him address the woman, and they see that the woman recognizes Jesus risen from the dead as he calls her gently by her name.

— ❀ —

The wise men are on their return journey. Baltazar is first to break the trio, so that he can travel home.

'Our visions have anticipated the fulfilment of the good God's promise,' Gaspar says. 'Let us give thanks for what is to come.'

Gaspar himself, after a long and eventful journey, takes his leave of Melchior, who continues farther to his home.

The star shines less brightly and is now no brighter than most others. The light of Christ born into the world now lightens the paths of these weary travellers to their customary dwellings.

What do they now? Do they prepare their kin for the missionaries who eventually will spread east? Do they return to the holy land to see in reality the future they have glimpsed? Do they allow the light of the Word made flesh to burn brilliantly in their lives? The story does not tell us, and yet it is likely that the wise men do what we know we should do, from this Christmas and always.

The Visions of the Innkeeper

The innkeeper did not, perhaps, feature in the Nativity of our Lord at all. But, for the purposes of this story, we shall assume he did and that his name was Isaac.

He sat, exhausted, on a rough-hewn bench, with Miriam, his wife, alongside. Dried figs and apricots, wine and bread were before them on the table. The inn was full – there were travellers resting even in part of their own quarters. Miriam had been compelled to gather her small children together on one mattress. The inn was a cluster of flat-topped dwellings, each dwelling, or part of it, hired to travellers from the east, west, north and south. Isaac had turned some away. There were travellers on their way to Jerusalem, travellers on their way from that great city. There was much movement and confusion in the whole land over the census imposed by the Roman authorities. Why, there was a census station only a short distance from the inn.

The inn itself nestled close to the foot of a sizeable hill, on which grazed a special flock of sheep whose lambs were used for temple sacrifice at Jerusalem. Around the foot of the hill curled the road from Hebron, a town thirteen miles to the south. Barren mountains almost encircled Bethlehem, but the six-mile passage north to Jerusalem was a much-cultivated green valley.

It was a pleasure to rest. Isaac did not let the authorities worry him too much; at least they left him to his business, a business that had been in his family for any number of generations. Miriam also was content to go about her duties without complaint. After all, the Jews had had a history of being under the heel of the foreigner. If they turned from the Most High God, what could they expect but punishment? However, it had been revealed to the great prophet Isaiah that, eventually, their nation would be restored by a child born in their midst and ultimately acclaimed 'the everlasting Father' and 'Prince of Peace' who would sit upon the throne of King David. What a miracle that would be! Isaac rubbed his lightly-bearded chin and recovered from his meditation, and smiled at his wife. 'Oh, you are still with us, then!' she exclaimed in good humour. He patted her hand and drained his cup. The tranquillity of the night was then shattered by a peremptory rap at the door.

Midnight callers were not unknown, but at least Isaac would be able to turn them away with an apologetic 'I'm sorry, we're full up', and then go to bed himself. As he opened the door, he saw that his visitors were not ordinary travellers. A middle-aged man stood holding a donkey upon which sat a young woman. The man enquired politely about accommodation and helped the young woman from the animal. Isaac was about to shake his head when he noticed that the woman was in the advanced stages of her pregnancy. By now, Miriam had brushed past her husband and was steadying the woman. 'The inn is full, but you must make use of our room.' The man graciously refused and, indicating the imminence of the birth, asked for a corner in even the meanest outhouse. Miriam was not happy at the prospect, but enquired of her husband, 'Could we not at least make them comfortable in the stabling? There's plenty of hay and clean straw.' Joseph said that he and his wife Mary would be content with such an arrangement.

At the foot of the hill was a large well-sheltered cavern, which was used for some livestock. It was a cold night but the couple would be warm there. As they entered, a bright star above the hill seemed to send a faint beam of light cascading to the entrance of the cave. Isaac removed hay from the centre of a small stack within, and made a shelter for the couple.

The donkey only reluctantly joined a rather grim-looking ox nearby, but soon seemed content. Miriam arrived with food and other provisions and, at a sign from Mary, she said to Isaac 'I shall look after her now: you'd better return to the children.' Isaac was relieved: it was no place for a man, he thought.

His mind returned to the prophets, and he smiled as he remembered Isaiah's 'for unto us a child is born'. He did not believe that the Most High God would lower himself in such a way. No, the promised one would come more splendidly. In those days bad men would be converted; evil men would refrain from sin and 'the calf and the young lion would lie in the straw' as the prophet put it. As he closed the door behind him, a shiver tripped delicately down his spine at the thought that God had always moved very mysteriously in history. A passage from the prophet Micah then sprang to mind: 'For out of thee, O Bethlehem, shall come a ruler in Israel'.

Miriam had not returned to the house: Isaac could not rest. Something intrigued him, but he did not know what. He went out into the cold again and, from a distance, looked across at the cave at the foot of the hill. The ray of light was now bright and distinct. The moon, however, was obscured by layers of cloud – some layers moving more quickly than others.

Was it over? Was it safe for him to venture towards the stabling? No, he'd give it a little while yet, he thought. He leaned against a hitching post and suddenly began to feel strange. His mind and eyes clouded momentarily, and then they cleared. It was daylight. He was still at the foot of a hill, it was true, but it was not his hill in Bethlehem. To his horror he recognized Golgotha, the hill of crucifixion outside Jerusalem. He pinched himself and slapped his face, but no one in the crowd noticed, commented or paid any attention. An execution procession was coming. Two men with their crosses were already being made to climb the hill – they were rough-looking villains, thought Isaac. Now came the rest of the sorry spectacle – a man much-abused, stumbling along the road with a head-dress of thorns pressed down upon his head, so that the thorns pierced his forehead and drew blood. Someone had been ordered to carry his cross. The prisoner was in physical agony. But there was something about him

Isaac could not quite put his finger on. The man was not an obvious criminal, and there were a few sympathetic followers who cried out to him and tried to comfort him but were driven back by the Roman guards shouting oaths and wielding whips and staves. It was an awful and pathetic sight. Many in the crowd were enjoying the spectacle: many were not. Who was this man?

When this pitiable figure had reached that part of the crowd in which Isaac found himself standing, the man stood upright and the crowd faded away; one of the female followers stood in front of him and both faced Isaac. The man had a short, forked beard and a face of much serenity: the woman was about fifty, with a face lined with grief. Her anxiety cleared a little as she said to Isaac: 'Thank you for your kindness and hospitality'. It was the girl now giving birth in his stable, but so much older and distraught. Was the man her son? Was it the child actually being born tonight? He shook his head and slapped his face again. He was leaning against the hitching post looking across at the cave. Was he mad? Was it a vision? Simple, ordinary men don't have visions. He said out loud: 'Who are these strangers? Why are they to suffer in this way?'

Some of the prophecies about the Messiah suggested that he would suffer for the redemption of the world, that his suffering would be a necessary part of his Messiahship. How would that be? Isaac did not understand. And what was the purpose of his being granted visions? He was stiff in the cold, and swung his arms about his body.

Still the starlight illuminated the entrance of the cave, and still the cloudy part of the sky shrouded the moon above the hillside. He decided to wait a little while longer before visiting the cave, and he returned to the house. His children were fast asleep. He could not rest; instead, he looked through the squint beside the door, out on to the hillside.

His senses became numb and he found himself sitting on another hillside – a green one with olive trees. Again he was with his wife in the midst of a large crowd seated around the same man Isaac had seen on his way to be crucified. He was preaching and teaching. He taught in parables as was the way with some teachers, but these parables were different somehow. Love seemed to be the foundation of a proper response to God: it went further than the letter of the law beloved of the Pharisees. You should love your enemies and those who despise you; do good to those who are against you. God should come first, not where and when it was convenient to put on a show. He talked of God as Father of all; he

28

forgave sins and healed the sick. Isaac's heart was gladdened. But at the back of the crowd he saw two or three known to him as temple officials, whispering conspiratorially. Clearly, this would lead to Jesus's destruction. They would not accept his words and would not listen: he would upset their world.

In one of his stories, Jesus likened God to the owner of a vineyard who sent his servants to collect rent from the tenants but, like the prophets, the servants were abused and cast out. Then the owner sent his son – his son the tenants would respect – but they killed him and fancied they would inherit the vineyard. Now Isaac could see more clearly. How, though, is mankind to be saved if its Saviour is led away to be crucified with robbers and murderers? On that hillside the crowd was not privy to his thoughts; it was a happy crowd, which had just eaten its fill. Isaac recognized some of the faces from the earlier vision. The hillside was bathed in sunlight; Isaac, however, did not feel the warmth of it. He found himself still peering through the squint, the vision gone.

Through the squint he could see that the hilltop was now bathed in moonlight; a gap in the cloud had revealed a more distant curtain of cloud, which, in turn, had broken and parted to reveal the moon in all its shimmering beauty. The moonbeams picked out the shepherd's hut and the flocks penned around the hut. Isaac stood up straight and could resist no longer the urge to see this miracle born so insignificantly on his land.

— ❀ —

Our innkeeper tentatively approached the entrance to his makeshift stable. The place was peaceful. The oxen were warm and quiet; the donkey wore an amused expression on its face but made no noise. Joseph had settled on a bundle of straw, apparently mending an old treadle lathe lately discarded by Isaac. Mary lay asleep, the child in her arms. Light seemed to hover over them. Miriam bustled about collecting various things to return to the house. 'Heaven be praised – some good work tonight; may the angels sing!' she said to Isaac, and he smiled tenderly at the Holy Family.

Mary awakened and Joseph leaned forward enquiringly. She gently laid the child on a woollen rug on top of the goats' manger, made sure the child was safe and secure, and returned to her slumber. Joseph, content that all was well, settled again to his task. Isaac thought he ought to go, but was overcome by that now familiar feeling. A terrible sight awaited him in his vision: our Blessed Lord crucified, high on the cross erected between those of the villains. His mother was at the foot of the cross, and clearly one of his disciples was with her. Others stood afar off. Racked with pain and in agony, he asked the disciple to be his mother's son and that they should look after one another. Satisfied, therefore, that they would comply, he cried out loudly as the sky darkened, and in anguish he died. The nails had pierced his wrists and his feet, and the crown of thorns still pressed firmly on his head. Above, Isaac saw three languages declaring: 'Jesus of Nazareth, King of the Jews'. The disciple and Mary embraced. Isaac watched through tearful eyes. He saw a soldier make sure of his death – with a spear. He saw a friend of Mary and a few others take down the body for burial, and for a moment saw the crucified Saviour's head cradled by his mother on her lap, using the same hand movements she had used when placing the child for the first time on the manger-bed. Isaac turned away to leave Mary to her grief and in doing so, found himself leaving the cave.

'They must move up to the house, Miriam,' Isaac announced after he had spoken emotionally of his visions. She clutched his arm and, overawed, could not speak.

Neither Isaac nor Miriam had any appetite for sleep.
They would allow the Holy Family to rest
undisturbed until morning but, in the meantime,
would prepare space within their own dwelling.
Isaac moved furniture in readiness, and Miriam
busied herself with other things. She glanced
anxiously at her husband from time to time. And
again he looked at the hillside through the squint.
Under the moonlight he thought he could make out
some figures descending the hillside, and mentioned
the fact to his wife. They were anxious that nothing
should disturb their guests.

Isaac rubbed his eyes and when he looked he
was once again on that fateful hillside outside
Jerusalem. Our Lord was on the cross, but no one
was at its foot. After he had closed his eyes for a
second or two in sorrow, Isaac found himself in the
middle of thronging crowds. A brilliant light was the
background to the cross, which now stood on its own
– not a thing of horror any more. In place of the
thorns there was a golden crown, much jewelled.
And fine garments graced our Lord's body. The
crowd fell on their faces as thunder rolled around the
hillside. A terrifying voice declared: 'This is my Son
in whom I am well pleased.' The cross was gradually
absorbed into the light and there remained a dove,
seemingly on fire, but the fire did not damage the
bird. The fiery dove flickered and became smaller so

that it formed the light of Isaac's oil lamp as he uncovered his face.

The visions were becoming stranger by the hour. 'This I cannot understand. What is here revealed? O God, why did you not choose a man of greater intellect?' he cried out loud.

'Isaac!' Miriam scolded. 'If God troubles to give the gift of visions and insights, he is not going to grant them to the wrong man.'

Isaac nodded and became less troubled, content that he would be able to understand all in God's good time.

He must now ensure that there was going to be no undue disturbance from the shepherds.

Isaac once more walked towards the stable: the pool of pale starlight still indicated the general area of holiness. As he drew near, three shepherds – two fairly old, one a youngster – scrambled towards him, breathlessly telling him an extraordinary tale, although on this night it did not strike Isaac as altogether extraordinary. The youngster carried a pet lamb over his shoulder as a gift for the child. The shepherds knelt in the straw. Mary was again holding the child; and Joseph had repaired Isaac's broken lathe, which was whirring away in perfect order. Joseph put the machine aside and clasped his hands, and perched himself above and behind Mary, who lay beside the manger smiling happily to her son. The oxen snorted contentedly and the donkey, well fed and exhausted, nodded its head, its legs crumpled underneath it on the floor. Somewhere above on a ledge, a dove fluffed its feathers. What a sight! About the Holy Family warm in the hay there seemed to be an aura of shimmering light.

Isaac gripped the framework of the wooden cladding at the cave's entrance: he was standing, unseen, in an upper room in Jerusalem. Around the low table lay a dozen men and Jesus himself, each supporting himself upon one elbow. Beside Jesus on the one side, Isaac recognized the disciple at the foot of the cross. 'This is my body,' Jesus said anon, as he broke bread and passed it to his friends, 'which is given for you: do this as often as you eat and drink.' It was a curious blessing to some of the disciples, but Isaac was aware of its significance - a significance both terrible and wonderful.

The upper room became the stable and the former scene prevailed. Isaac looked behind him to see Miriam and his young sons trotting along the path from the house to see what had to be seen. 'Out of the mouths of babes ... '

Benjamin, at five the eldest of the three, tugged at his father's robe and said in the piercing tone of a child: 'That's God's son over there, you know.'

The older shepherds had told our innkeeper that there was evidence of a fairly large encampment a few miles north of the city – travellers from Jerusalem, but originally from much farther afield.

'If they are encamped it is unlikely that they will require our services,' Isaac reassured his wife as they helped Mary, Joseph and the child move into the comfort of the house. Mary rested her hand upon Isaac's forearm and said gently: 'Thank you for your kindness and hospitality'. And he remembered the grim procession to Golgotha.

As Isaac wondered about kindness and love, that same cloak of the future was drawn over him. Our Lord was resting on the sand. A woman was before him. He was drawing carelessly in the sand as three stalwarts of the temple and of the letter of the law were questioning him.

'What would you do with this vile woman?' they asked. 'She is an adulteress. She must be stoned to death according to the book of the laws.'

'Yes, perhaps that is so,' replied Jesus still drawing in the sand 'but first think, and then proceed, with the sinless man among you casting the first stone at this woman.' They coughed nervously, muttered and, one by one, shuffled away, conscious for the first time of their own shortcomings. The woman stood, terrified.

'Where are your accusers?' he asked her gently.

'They are gone.'

'And neither do I condemn you. Go on your way, and sin no more.'

Justice, generosity, loving kindness, forgiveness and mercy are the important ingredients in his perfection – all the attributes of God revealed over the ages, thought Isaac. And the scene became a garden of rest, with a sepulchre before him. It was open, the stone door having been thrust aside. The woman Isaac recognized from the vision just gone, was standing weeping beside the tomb. Suddenly there was a figure beside her. She was addressing him as if he were the gardener. 'They have taken the body of my Lord. Where have they put it?' Isaac saw the figure turn and say gently: 'Mary'. It was the Lord, risen from the dead.

That evening, travellers from the encampment arrived at the house. Three fine, wealthy, richly-dressed, exotic travellers, and their attendants. The bright star now seemed to aim its shaft of light on to the house. Through interpreters they told our innkeeper and his wife of their journey; and then presented the child with gifts.

'Gold for a king,' Isaac commented 'incense for a God, and myrrh for a mortal. Because for sure, he is all three.'

Our innkeeper rubbed his lightly-bearded chin as he pondered the sights and visions he had been granted. This child would be no warrior-king but a priestly Messiah, the Son of God, who would swallow death and so draw all mankind to him. And 'all mankind' would include Jew and non-Jew, for had he not now been shown to the whole world through the agency of a trio of foreigners?

For the last time Isaac was driven for a few moments from current reality. At first he saw a palace comprising many mansions, rather as in the manner of his own inn, but grander. But there before him was the whole congregation of saints – holy men and women, who had simply fulfilled their God-given vocations, and there were martyrs, confessors, priests and doctors of the Church, matrons and those who had devoted their lives to God, all confessors of the true Faith. A brilliant light surrounded our Lord Christ, crowned and enthroned beside that which Isaac's eyes could not see for the glory of it. On his right hand was his mother Mary crowned and in splendour. His hands bore the marks of the nails. Before his breast there hovered the fiery dove, the Holy Spirit. His Apostles were with him. Angels and Archangels, Cherubim and Seraphim continually sang; their singing mingled with the incense of many censers as they prayed for those upon earth and for the souls journeying towards heaven: 'on earth, peace to men of good will'. The brilliance of the light began to blind Isaac and he found it then to fade and become but the full moon shining upon him. He made the sign on his body of the points of the holy cross. He returned to the bosom of his family, to await the unfolding mystery.

The Visions of Herod the Great and the Servant-Girl

This is the story of the visions of Herod the Great and those of a servant-girl. The story is not, as far as we know, factual, yet it may help to convey the truth about the Christmas message, and the truth of the Gospel. As we all now know, the birth of our Lord was probably a few years earlier than the calculations of former times suggest – between four and seven years earlier. We know that Herod the Great died in 4BC. He was a Jew, but not of pure stock. He was placed and supported on the throne by the Romans in return for keeping the country subdued at what was then the farthest corner to the east in the Roman Empire.

Herod was not entitled 'the Great' without cause. No, he possessed a splendid palace, with straight walls, flat and domed roofs, and a fine columned courtyard. Oh! he was truly king. The people knew who was master. Had he not killed even his wife Mariamne and, for that matter, one of his sons? There was no sentiment in King Herod. He was strong and masterful, and yet vulnerable and fearful.

On this day he paced his marbled retreat in an inner chamber. He was much troubled; his advisers had warned him of a portent, and his messengers had told him of a huge train of foreigners on camels making their way towards Jerusalem. He paced, wrapping and rewrapping a cloak about him. He was relatively safe on the throne; the Romans would see to that. And the Jews thought him preferable to the Romans. Nevertheless, he was troubled. He beat those who brought him news he could not suffer, and his fears were fuelled by constant dreams. He suspected everyone of treachery; that was why a wife and son lay dead. He paced again, then clutched at a rare and slender marble column whose delicate pink and green veins marked its length – a recent gift from Rome to gladden his palace. A little sunlight intruded where it could and caught the column beside Herod's eyes. He squinted; his grey-bearded face looked in torment. He closed his eyes and saw a man strangely apparelled, a prisoner in purple with a ring of thorns about his head, standing before one of Herod's own sons, Herod Antipas. Some of the thorns had pierced the man's forehead. Herod heard a bystander say to another: 'It is said he is the true King of the Jews – but not of this world'. Herod opened his eyes and tore the vision from his mind, angry and confused.

Herod knew all about the prophets. He knew that people expected a Saviour; as long as it did not interfere with his own ambitions, all was well. However, he was now receiving information from his messengers that the travellers from the East were intent upon searching for a child they believed was the King of Kings. Was it sheer nonsense? Anyway, he was safe enough, because he had had a further vision beside that same column and he had seen the prisoner again, about to be lifted high upon a cross. Herod had laughed and had clapped his hands in glee. So if the child and prisoner were one and the same, he would eventually die, and therefore would be of no threat to the dynasty which he, Herod, had begun. Herod lay back on his couch elated, ready for food and pleasures to excess.

The servant-girl, Rachel, was proud to be a servant to Herod the Great. He, of course, did not know that she existed. Indeed, she had never set eyes upon the King and was only a servant of a servant. She lived in a hovel not far from the palace with her father and mother, who also acted as menials. But the family was free. She had been brought up well in the rudiments of her religion. She had high hopes of the prophets. But she honoured the idea of King Herod, the notion of kingship, and she longed to enter the palace and into his presence. There had been many tales about him, and yet

41

Rachel did not believe a king could be anything but worthy.

Jerusalem was in turmoil. Roman soldiers were rushing about everywhere setting up census booths for tax registration, and there were many strangers. There were, in fact, rumours of Eastern travellers carrying wealth and exotic goods – all because of an unusually bright star in the night sky, which cast its light a little way south of Jerusalem. Rachel's main interest and aim was to insinuate herself into the very shadow of the great Herod. She spent her day performing duties, duties the principal servants found distasteful. On this day, by stealth and persistence, she found herself behind the marble column and in front of Herod's special retreat. Oddly, there was no one about save the King himself and an attendant serving some refreshment. The King was angry: but what a magnificent sight – the black and grey hair, the grey beard, the pride and the vanity. The luckless attendant was sent sprawling to the floor.

She coughed involuntarily and, as the attendant picked himself up and left, so Herod rose and stumped towards the column, which was now beginning to intrigue him to the extent that he found it irresistible. Rachel cowered.

But Herod was too concerned with himself and
the intriguing visions. He paused at the pillar and
yelled: 'Oh Great God, show me now how the
usurper meets his end!' What was the King saying?
Rachel could not understand. Why was he calling
upon God in that angry way? She was steadying
herself against the column as Herod himself was
doing on the other side. The edge of his cloak crept
round the pillar and touched the servant-girl. She
started. At the same time Herod was entranced by
the sunlight and in reverie. The sunlight seemed to
curl around the pillar as the cloak had done; it
caressed Rachel's hand. They both saw a man on a
hillside with crowds at his feet; they heard him
called 'Jesus'; they saw the crowd hang on his every
word; they saw miracles of healing of mind and
body; they saw the poor strengthened and the selfish
warned; they saw ... Herod recognized the man:
Rachel, of course, did not. Herod cried out at his own
frustration; he did not wish to be subjected to this; he
desired to see this man dead on the cross, to make
sure that there was nothing to fear for the future of
his dynasty. He did not wish to see this. He forced
himself away from the pillar. Rachel was not
conscious of Herod. This Jesus possessed such
authority, yet he had humility. He was a man, yet
Godlike. The vision became unclear as the sun's ray
failed, and Rachel became aware of the marble and
heard the sound of the raging King. She was

unsettled: she was excited at seeing King Herod at last in all his outward magnificence and yet she confessed disappointment to herself, not because he was noisy and violent, but because he was after all rather ordinary. On the other hand, this peculiar vision so attracted her. What was it telling her? And, anyway, who sees visions these days?

It was now clear that the travellers were intent upon seeking advice from Herod himself, and his messengers gave regular reports of their progress towards Jerusalem. Herod's own seers and philosophers had themselves pointed to the bright star as some sort of omen, whether good or bad they were at first reluctant to say.

The servant-girl, far outside the palace wall, cleaned the things the principal servants would not clean. In her work she pondered the curious events and determined to return to the palace, to that inner place where she could secretly learn more about the nature of her monarch and ruler. However, she longed to return to that hillside and the adoring crowds. Cleverly, she again found her way undetected: this time there were messengers in conference with the mighty Herod. Rachel was even more wary of capture and a beating, as she watched from behind that same marble pillar. She tentatively rested her hand on the column and hoped and waited – nothing. She could still hear the voices further on. A tear of disappointment … Her watery eyes found it difficult to focus: then what she saw became clearer – not the floor of Herod's palace but a plain earthen floor, whitewashed walls and a single narrow window. Through the window burst glorious light, and a young woman knelt before it. A voice from the light declared to this young woman – Mary, he called her – what God had planned for her; that she would bear a child of the Most High, named Jesus. Mary stood and said simply: 'Let it be as God wills', and the scene faded from view.

Rachel removed herself from the presence of Herod's court.

Herod had invited the travellers to his palace. Clearly they required some help, which he would give them. After all, he was a great king, whose greatness was renowned. If the light in the sky told the travellers of a divine king newly born into the world, he was in a position to tell them that God had disclosed the downfall and death to follow this miraculous birth.

But he resolved to keep that to himself for the time being. He paced. He was angry one moment, and calm the next. He made an outburst one moment, and was engaged in gentle conversation the next. He paced, and then paused beside the familiar column, treated now by him almost with awe and respect, which, in Herod, qualified for humility. He leaned against it. There was a rustle from behind the pillar but he took no notice.

Immediately, he was engulfed in darkness by an eclipse of the sun. There was an eerie silence. He heard gentle sobbing, perhaps from behind the pillar, but, no, it couldn't be; no, from an old woman in the arms of a young man at the foot of a cross. The crucified man had commended his mother to his friend; he had cried out a few words of despair and had died, his body racked in pain and bleeding. There were crosses on either side but the men thereon were still alive and writhing.

With joy, Herod removed himself from the vision and into his world. He roared for wine and drank a cup in one draught. 'So he will die for presuming too much. This is the great God's way of revealing to me that I have nothing to fear from the search of the travellers.' He drank again and cuffed the steward, with another roar of delight. Behind the column, the servant-girl lay in a crumpled devastated heap. Her vision had been identical with

Herod's so far, but she was being urged to concentrate further. She saw the horrific sight again, the sorrow of Mary, the hideous death of the man on the hillside. Why? The more she concentrated, the lighter the sky became, and a large white cloud, almost like a hand, seemed to support the cross. A white dove hovered alongside. The figure on the cross was no longer broken and bent. His face was strong but of gentle expression. His head was no longer crowned with thorns but with a crown of pure gold.

— ❀ —

So he shall be a king, she realized, and shall reign from the cross. The jigsaw was not yet complete but Rachel was sure of the regal triumph of Jesus over death. But when was he born? When is he to be born and where?

She was again at her tasks, ever dutiful but no longer under any illusions about man's idea of power, glory and strength.

Herod rubbed his hands with glee. He had given a splendid banquet the night before. No one knew why his spirits were so high. But all knew well the adage: 'Laugh when he laughs; leave, if you can, before he snarls.' But he was Herod the Great, and a welcome buffer between the Jews and the Romans. Herod was still in a fine mood. He longed to see the travellers and gloat obscurely at them.

God's plan has been revealed to us already, Rachel thought, as she pondered the prophet's words taught to her from infancy. There must, however, be more to it than a picture of triumph over a tragic scene. She shuddered at the memory of a mother devastated at the death of her son, shoulders rigid in anguish. But had the prophets not foretold that the Messiah would also be the suffering servant of all?

That night she peered in at the fire from the threshold of her dwelling. No longer did she require the contrast of an opulent palace. The visions would continue to visit her wherever she was. At first she could not distinguish between reality and dream. It was dark. But the darkness was pierced by the light of one star, which had appeared in the sky a few weeks before. She saw a stable in a hillside cave, straw and animals, warm against the frosty night, and in the manger, hay. She saw the mother Mary, exhausted, resting on a bed of straw, an older man beside her; an indifferent ox munching, eyed warily by a donkey; a lamb, dropped by a group of shepherds visiting this natural spectacle, settling in the straw. She saw a man and woman – Rachel recognized Isaac and Miriam, innkeepers of Bethlehem – appearing with fruit and bread, and a light shining from the manger.

Rachel stood and looked out at the cold night, in the direction of Bethlehem and the bright star above. It dawned upon her that the birth had occurred that very night, and she longed to be there.

The travellers had arrived at the palace – three fine rich men, the favourites of their respective kings, all bound for the same place. They required directions to Bethlehem where they believed a new king would be or had been born.

Herod paced excitedly. He would enjoy this meeting. He'd send for them in a moment. He drank a draught of wine and leaned against the customary pillar and quickly removed his hand, then grinned at his own foolishness and pressed his hand firmly on the marble, confident in the knowledge that his family's position was assured in perpetuity.

The palace was gone: a hillside cemetery replaced it. A woman stood outside an open sepulchre, weeping. She was not far from the figure of a man whose face Herod could not see. He heard the woman say, 'They have taken away my Lord' and the man reply, 'Mary'. Then the man lifted his head and looked straight at Herod. Herod shook his head, roared, threw his golden cup across the decorated floor, and roared again. For ten minutes he raged, then stopped and smiled an almost angelic smile. 'Of course! God is warning me what will happen if this child is allowed to live. I shall use the travellers to seek him, then I shall kill him and so preserve my name.'

It had not been difficult for Rachel to persuade the many attendants to the wise men to accommodate her for the six miles or so to Bethlehem. On the way she experienced further dreams and nightmares: the beauty of our Lord's calm and devastatingly simple words, the gentleness of spirit, the evil men first in the background and then in the foreground encouraging the crowd to yell, 'Crucify! Crucify!': the stumbling, bent figure under the weight of the cross, the bleeding shoulder, the constant whipping; the final stumble, and the impatient Roman soldier compelling a young man to carry the cross for the broken figure. There in Bethlehem, where now Rachel was, the Holy Family had removed to the innkeeper's own house. There Rachel stood as the wise men gave absurd gifts for a child – but gold for a king, incense for a God, and myrrh for a mortal.

And in Jerusalem Herod was angry. The travellers had deceived him and had not returned with details of the birth: another chalice of wine was cast to the floor, another son was killed, another steward beaten. Herod called his armiger to arrange the slaughter of all young children in the region of Bethlehem to ensure that the usurper was killed and no more a threat to Herod's dynastic aspirations. All this death in vain: the innkeeper would send the Holy Family on their way to safety in Egypt before the slaughter began.

Rachel, now returned to Jerusalem, wished to brave and risk, for the last time, the inside of Herod's palace. Again she succeeded without detection. The nature of kingship now fascinated her. Herod was engrossed in his fury. His mind brimmed with the way this man Jesus defied the Romans, his own son Antipas and even death itself. 'He will return and live in this very palace!' he cried out in despair. He stumbled and supported himself against the column, and now Rachel was standing before the great man himself. But Herod could not see her; his eyes were glazed. They both saw the power and the light of God the Father surround the heavenly throne where Jesus was seated, a holy dove hovering before. They heard and saw choruses of celestial messengers praising this Holy Trinity, with the mother Mary seated beside, interceding with the saints and martyrs for all souls, all the host of them in a joyful, now-fading vision. As the sacrifice of Jesus as a means of redemption of the whole world gradually revealed itself to Rachel, she looked boldly at Herod and left the palace without subterfuge. Herod stood, rigid and in torment.

The Visions of the Centurion

Let us suppose that Gaius was the centurion who witnessed the crucifixion, who was responsible for the gruesome detail of the day's crucifixions, and who uttered the words recorded in the Gospel, 'Truly this man was the Son of God', as he witnessed the death of Jesus. What an odd thing for the centurion to say! What might have been the reason?

Gaius was in charge of one hundred men. His was the burden of a captain, but probably his was the social standing of a sergeant-major. Imagine, then, the scene confronting this centurion. It was a scene largely of his own making, for Gaius was in charge. Most of the work had by now been done; it remained only to make sure of the deaths of the two robbers and the curious man in between, above whose head the governor Pontius Pilate had insisted a plaque be hung with the words 'Jesus of Nazareth – King of the Jews'. But they had crowned him with thorns, not gold.

Gaius was a short muscular man. He wore his badge of rank with pride – his uniform of leather. He had thrust his short, broad dagger into the vital organs of many a barbarian; he had urged his men to be ruthless; he had won promotion and made his name in terrible battles. He was proud of the Empire as it pushed its boundaries ever further to enclose lands of the uncivilized peoples – not that the Jews were in any way uncivilized. They had a fine and ancient culture respected by Rome. Had Rome not allowed the Jews largely to govern themselves by the sons and descendants of Herod the Great? Of course, when the Jews offended against Roman authority, and even when the Jews asked for Roman justice – as was the case with Jesus of Nazareth – then the governor would administer that justice on behalf of Caesar. Today there were three sentences being executed. Pontius Pilate had magnanimously asked the Jews if they would wish the governor to release Jesus, at this sacred time for the Jews. They asked for Barabbas, a seditious murderer. Gaius had seen the Chief Priests encourage the fickle crowds to yell, 'Crucify him!' when offered Jesus's freedom. But what did Gaius care? He wasn't a Jew. He'd seen so many trials and had taken charge of many crucifixions. He was battle-hardened and inured to the dying groans and grieving moans of the friends and relations. He had never been moved by displays of affection and emotion. He remained aloof. But when his daughter would clutch his leg and beg him not to leave and go about his duties, his heart would soften as he patted the child's head and pushed her away towards her mother without a word.

Now it was uncannily dark as time was running out for the three men on the crosses. At the foot of the middle cross was a female figure; Gaius took it to be the mother of Jesus. She looked up at her son, her shoulders tense in grief, and then momentarily turned and glanced at Gaius. In the second or so he caught her glance, he felt an unwonted feeling of guilt mingled with sadness, anger and, unaccountably, love. He was able to discern these feelings though the experience was as a flash of lightning. He then found himself not on that awful hill of crucifixion.

Where was he? Ah, he recognized the Mount of Olives, on the other side of the Kidron Valley. Here was Jesus surrounded by his disciples, teaching. He taught them of God in terms quite different from other rabbis and teachers. Gaius had always admired the God of the Jews – always so much more evident than the Roman gods, although he was never drawn or carved. The Roman gods only existed as the work of skilled craftsmen. He, quite honestly, had little time for them, though, by law, he was obliged to

worship them. But he had gradually been persuaded
by the God of the Jews who, they said, was the only
God, anyway. It all fitted Gaius's idea of a grand
design. Yet here was Jesus of Nazareth talking with
such authority and command about God. Gaius was
captivated. But why was he here? He had never
experienced this man's preaching before: this was no
trick of memory. He was accustomed to blood and
death and matters easily explained. He was losing
his grip and shook his head violently, and there he
was back on the hill of death. Had he felt faint? He
must not show any weakness in front of his men. He
had a reputation. He took a few paces backwards.

Gaius knew that the Jewish religion looked to a
time when God would send a Saviour. That Saviour
would, presumably, be a warrior-king; and this man
dying on the cross was in no position to be such a
king. And yet he knew the prophets had foretold that
in the days of the promised Saviour the deaf would
hear and the blind would see. Certainly rumour had
it that Jesus cured both these afflictions among others.
Furthermore, the prophets had foretold a suffering
servant of all, and, in fact, Jesus had been explaining
that very scripture on the Mount of Olives.

The mother of Jesus turned briefly to Gaius and
he tried to avert his gaze. He failed, and the mixture
of emotions struck him as a cold plunge in the bath
house. Again, he was elsewhere.

The soldiers, as was their custom, threw dice for the clothing of the dying men. The thieves muttered; occasionally Jesus spoke; already the soldiers had given him some sour wine to relieve his suffering. They saw their captain a little way off in rapt attention. But in reality Gaius was elsewhere.

He was on the threshold of a small room, earthen floor, whitewashed walls – ordinary enough, not unlike his own dwelling. A young woman was folding linen. It was a normal domestic scene, a scene acted throughout the land. Then a sun's ray coincided with the small window, and the brilliant light flooded the room. Again, ordinary enough – yet not so, because, when the young woman turned towards the light, a voice called out, 'Mary!' As she turned, Gaius saw the grieving mother thirty or forty years younger. Her features were unlined and perfect. The voice declared the extraordinary, if not outrageous, proposition that Mary was to become the mother of the 'Son of God'. She acquiesced in the face of a demand the consequences of which she could not possibly know. This selfless acceptance was equal in measure to her steadfastness at the cross as the young woman replied 'Be it unto me according to thy word'.

The cries of the thieves intruded. The visions twisted and turned in his mind. Visions? Only generals, who can afford rich spices from the East,

see visions. He withdrew his short sword and
slapped the side of his leg to cause himself some
pain, with the intention of bringing himself to his
senses. The noise was enough to cause Mary to look
at him again as she was comforted by a disciple of
Jesus. And once more Gaius was transported.

— ✤ —

What did all this mean? Why me? he asked almost
out loud, checking himself in time. Irrationally, he
longed for the security of the gods Jupiter and Mars;
at least he could not believe in them.

Mary's glance had sent him to an inn on the
outskirts of a town. It did not appear quite as he
knew it, but he was aware it was Bethlehem, five or
six miles from Jerusalem. It was a cold night and
everything was illuminated by the moon and a
particularly bright star. At the door of the inn he saw
an older man who had led there a donkey upon
which was seated the young woman of the earlier
vision. Gaius recalled with delight that near this inn
his father had set up a census station many years
before when he, Gaius, was but two or three. Yes,
Isaac was the innkeeper at that time, he remembered.
He remembered further that there had been an
amazing family scene in the stable of the inn, where

a woman had given birth to a boy. Had his father not also talked about crowds of foreigners visiting the inn?

He could not hear much of the conversation at the inn door, but it appeared that the elderly man did not desire any special treatment because the inn was full. He was grateful to be shown a corner of the cave at the foot of the nearby hill. There was now no doubt in Gaius's mind what was unfolding. But how could the Son of the Most High be born in a stable? What a strange and perverse God was the God of the Jews!

In a moment of detachment he appreciated the irony of it.

Again that grim hillside, where he now watched what he had often watched, but never before with the feeling that he was not the master of the scene. From this his duty he had been thrown into another world where the sequences of time and history were disobedient. He longed for the order of the regiment, the rules and the regulations, for orders he could read, understand and act upon. O to be relieved of this burden! but it was a burden placed upon him by the hand of some omnipotence.

With instructions from the cross Jesus had made sure his disciple, John, would take care of his mother. There was something remarkable about that. There had also been something remarkable about the fact, as Gaius now recalled, that as the huge and ugly nails were fixing this man to the cross, he had said: 'Father, forgive them'. Are all men capable of that? Gaius wondered.

Mary turned away from the disciple, kissed her son's feet and returned to her comforter; in doing so, her face etched with torment again caught the centurion's stare. In despair he cried out in his mind. The life of this preacher, this teacher, this miracle worker, this Son of God imprisoned in humanity, is being thrown away by his Creator and Father, used and cast aside. To what end? But this was not the end.

On a hillside bathed in sunlight (the side favoured by the Jews for burial) Gaius stood, not far from a tomb freshly sealed with a large stone. Two of his soldiers guarded it. The same brilliant light he had seen pouring into that small room and lighting the night sky in Bethlehem caused the two soldiers to fall and sleep. The light obliterated the tomb for a moment. He saw some women walking towards the tomb whose stone now had miraculously been rolled aside. He could see that there was no corpse inside. The centurion caught his breath, and now some way off he saw Jesus standing, talking gently to another woman he, Gaius, had seen on the crucifixion hill, who could not raise her eyes through grief until she recognized Jesus when he called her by name. His wrists and hands bore the marks of the nails and ropes, his feet likewise.

It was dark again, and Gaius looked at Mary.

His station on the dark hillside was now as observer of the majesty of God, who by his love of mankind was prepared to give his Son up to the will of man, for the salvation of mankind. Gaius moved to place himself in line with the middle cross; no longer did he fear the face of Mary and what it might reveal. This time he gladly found himself watching three shepherds outside the cave where were stabled some animals, and where the Holy Family rested. The youngest shepherd carried a lamb, which dropped to the floor and sank into the straw. The three of them had been frightened by the brilliance of the starlight, and spoke of a heavenly message directing them to this place. As Gaius looked at Mary, the newborn child, and the husband and guardian, Joseph, he marvelled at the revelation of these weighty matters not only to himself but originally to these simple shepherds from the hillside.

Yet Gaius's foreknowledge of the Resurrection did not diminish his growing horror of the scene before him. This was the result of man's selfishness, greed and self-love in which he, Gaius, had played a significant part. And the shame of it overcame him, that stout and steady soldier. But Mary's face had transported him again to Bethlehem, though this time to the living quarters of Isaac and Miriam where Mary and the young child had been accommodated. There was much commotion. There were travellers, fine travellers from rich free lands far off. By report, they were wise men seeking in the wisdom of the stars a newborn Prince of the world, whose birth was predicted by the light of the bright star shining on Bethlehem. The men dismounted and Isaac was happy to lead them to the Holy Family. The wise men knelt. Gaius smiled at God's complete embrace by revealing his Son to simple folk and then to splendid foreigners. His Son was here for both Jew and Gentile – for the whole of mankind.

Their gifts were grander than the shepherds' gifts. However, Gaius was struck by the significance of the gifts – gold for a king, incense for a God, and myrrh for a mortal. Certainly the child was all three.

The great God had given him a precious glimpse of what had been and what was to come. But why? What was God's purpose? From this point he understood that the gruesome sight of the man and the pitifully sad sight of the mother were terrible but necessary facets in place from the beginning of time.

With the dying words of Christ, 'It is accomplished: the work is finished', Gaius began to see that the Son of God would indeed absorb and conquer death, that, lifted high on the cross, raised from the dead, he would draw all men to himself, and would redeem mankind, because nailed to the cross with Jesus was the burden of the sin of mankind.

'Truly this man was the Son of God!' the centurion uttered out loud. And Mary turned.

The scene was again the stable in the cave: the wise men were still some way off. This time Gaius was inside, very close to a donkey, which did not notice him, of course. An ox appeared to grin but probably did not. Was he actually there? Which was the dream? The scene was comfortable: the child in the arms of his mother; Joseph, who had turned his hand to repairing an old treadle-lathe; the bustling wife of

Isaac busying herself with provisions and so forth;
the distant sound of rustics, the shepherds bringing
their friends to pay their respects, and to bring
another sheepskin or some other basic necessity. The
joy of the angels had filled them as they arrived once
more, quieting themselves as they did so. They
muttered rumours of the wise men – a great caravan
of camels coming this way. Miriam, still bustling,
insisted the family move to a proper bed in the
morning. The star shone without; and within, Mary
placed the child Jesus in a manger of hay. The upper
parts of the woodwork of the manger were proud of
the contents, and the lantern standing on the floor
projected onto the opposite wall the corner of the
structure as a huge, flickering, brooding, embracing
cross. And, as Mary placed the child in the manger,
for a second or so Gaius was confronted again by the
sight of the crucified Saviour. The projection stopped
flickering, the body on the cross became distinct. He
wore not thorns but a crown of gold and fine
vestment of gold. Around his feet clamoured joyful
folk from every walk of life: the former poor, the
former rich, the educated, the uneducated, all having
fulfilled what God had called them to do. The joy
was ecstatic and infectious, wholesome and glorious.
The projection flickered and became indistinct,
though Mary now caught sight of the shadow of the
cross and an instantaneous look of anguish passed
across her eyes. Her smile returned, and the lantern

was removed by a shepherd, who sat in its place. The scene was again happy contentment.

From a ledge above the cave wall fluttered a dove, which came to rest upon the manger.

The Visions of Lydia

Lydia was a sister to Lysia and sister also to four brothers, the youngest of whom was James. In fact, James was the youngest of the whole family. They were, if you consult the obscure, non-canonical *The History of Joseph and the Death of Joseph*, the children of the widower, Joseph, who became the husband of Mary and guardian of our Lord. Lydia was a devoted daughter, dark-haired and vivacious – perhaps rather too vivacious for the preference of Joseph, a quiet, religious man, an architect and a worthy carpenter. But Lydia was a dutiful daughter. She did not entirely make sense of her father's becoming engaged to a woman scarcely older, if at all, than herself. A woman, a girl indeed, who had at first been set aside for a special life in the precinct of the Temple at Jerusalem.

Lydia's mother had died when James was but in early infancy. Sad though it was, Joseph had done all a father could do, indeed, so much so that his friends and clients would mock him gently about woman's work. But Mary, that pious young lady, at the recommendation of the Temple officials, had helped enormously. Marriage had not been the original intention, and so the engagement was a surprise to most.

Joseph had kinsmen in Jerusalem and indeed in Bethlehem, about six miles away, the city of his birth. And so it was another surprise that Joseph and part of the family moved north to Nazareth, the distance of a few days' tedious journey in fact, even though it was Mary's home town. And now to Mary's childhood home Lydia was paying a visit with Mary. On the way, Lydia marvelled at the sight of the sheep and the goats, the simple things, the workshops, and the people who used their God-given talents to his glory. And she gave thanks for the whole of creation.

Mary's parents, Joachim and Anne, enjoyed old age in the customary flat-roofed, rounded-arched, rendered and plastered white building, much in common with its neighbours. Joseph had business in Jerusalem, and Mary and Lydia would therefore stay in Joachim's house for a short time with young James, and take the opportunity to collect gifts for the new household. In the linen-room, Mary gathered items of apparel and other cloth. Lydia, joking and laughing with Mary, then left the room to show Anne a piece of material 'too fine and valuable' in Mary's words, for her to take from her childhood home and away from her parents. Lydia paused to fold again this cloth, outside the only door of the room. The door was left ajar. An odd light began to shine from the room and the cloth she was holding appeared to glow. She giggled nervously at the strangeness of it and put her head on one side in the hope that she would understand the phenomenon a little better. Then she heard from within the room a kind voice of gentle authority. 'Fear not, Mary!' How could there be someone else in the room? she had left Mary alone, and had left by the only door. 'Do not be afraid: the Lord is with you,' the voice reassured. Lydia heard the announcement, and wondered. She knew her scripture of course: she was aware of the prophecies, of people's hopes. But how could Israel's hopes be realized in her circle of acquaintance and family?

Still the cloth in her hands glowed: and the passage of time seemed suspended.

There Lydia stood still, as did time – or so it appeared. The strange messenger was still in conversation with Mary. She felt she ought to feel ashamed at her eavesdropping, yet at the same time she knew she was there for a purpose. But to Lydia was slowly revealed the answer to her question, in advance of the unfolding of the Divine Plan. The cloth shone in her hands and she stared hard. She felt herself disappear into the cloth, and all around the sparkling hoar-frost was caught in the light of an unusually brilliant star. Mary and Lydia's father were making their way from Jerusalem, to travel the road to Bethlehem. Lydia knew the road well. Mary was obviously in the advanced stages of pregnancy and riding on a donkey the few miles to the City of David, the city of Joseph's birth. But why were they there?

Lydia stared as the regretful innkeeper and his wife directed the couple to a stable at the foot of a small hill not many yards away.

How would it be if the promised Messiah were to be born here among cattle and roosting birds? A humble Messiah? A humble Saviour, not grand and in splendour? Was that not a contradiction? But then Lydia saw another splendour, a deeper splendour: the splendour of simplicity and the grandeur of the hillside, of the beast of the field; truly the cradle of creation. But from this beginning how would he fulfil his Messiahship?

These visions were compressed into a few moments. Indeed, had not the minute or so been returned to her? She distinctly heard again the words: 'Fear not, Mary!' She could go quickly to Anne with the cloth and pretend none of it had occurred. Still the cloth glowed as if it were urging her to receive and understand the answers to her questions. Was this the stuff of which kings were made? What would be the nature of his kingship? Mankind had speculated often enough, and the Saviour was always to be a powerful warrior-king. To Lydia's surprise, the cloth left her hands, and her hands were revealed as aged hands, wrinkled and gnarled. It was fairly dark: she was out-of-doors somewhere. She looked up and was confronted by the hideous prospect of a crucifixion. In horror she saw Mary, elderly and grief-stricken, at the foot of the crucified man. Who was he? And her eyes rose apprehensively to study the contorted figure, bearded and naked save for a fine cloth hanging from his waist. A cruel mocking circle of thorns had been pressed upon his head, and above that wounded, dying head were words that made Lydia cry out loud, aghast: 'Jesus of Nazareth, King of the Jews' written in Hebrew, Latin and Greek. 'This then is his kingship?' she addressed God angrily. But no, there was more to it than that.

When she turned her gaze again to the cloth, now restored to her young hands, she was on the hillside alone. The effulgent glow of the cloth filled that hillside, and the cross, that instrument of torture and death, actually looked grand and majestic, but she could not focus upon Jesus for the brilliance of the light. The fine cloth was still in her hands and she sank to her knees as the shock of the first scene overcame her. How was it possible for the Saviour to redeem and save if his end was thus? Her young mind hardly coped. At the same time she heard Mary ask: 'How shall this be?' from within the linen-room.

Lydia knew that she must now seek further. The cloth became another hillside, this time under bright sun. Jesus, his face animated but under no strain, was preaching and teaching to a large crowd, a simple message, quite extraordinary in its simplicity, in fact. The crowd listened to the parables and gladly heard his word. But a small group of temple officials in the background looked menacing in their conspiracy. Did they feel threatened by his message? Why should they? Were they too sophisticated to understand?

The cloth was now the dry sandy soil. Jesus was drawing and writing in the sand. Some of his followers stood behind him. Scribes and Pharisees brought a struggling woman to him and threw her down on his writing. 'This woman we found committing adultery. The law says she ought to be taken away and stoned to death.' They sounded as though they were testing him for some reason. They willed him to contradict the law.

'Yes, you are quite right, that is what the law says: therefore carry on, and let the man without any sin at all throw the first stone at her.' They shuffled away awkwardly. 'Does no one condemn you?' he asked the frightened woman. 'Neither do I condemn you. Go and sin no more.'

Ignorant of all that was happening to his sister and indeed to his dear companion Mary, James toddled in to the passageway from the principal part of the house brandishing a cup he had broken. Lydia, startled out of her transportation, said crossly that it was too bad; and he enquired if it mightn't only be one bad as the cup was cracked anyway! Lydia sent him away with a flea in his ear and immediately regretted it. But even such studied innocence could not inhibit the revelations, and Lydia saw many children, anxious to see Jesus, being turned away by well-meaning disciples. 'No, no, do not discourage them. You can learn a lot from the innocence of a child. Only in that way can you gain entry into the Kingdom of Heaven.' Before him dumb men spoke and blind men saw – just as Isaiah has prophesied.

His message went right to the core. Lydia could see the uniqueness: she could see why he might be condemned to death as a consequence of the clever scribes and Pharisees. They guarded their own position jealously. But how would such a death, or any death for that matter, be an essential ingredient in the Divine Plan? How would his teaching spread? She folded and refolded the cloth in her hands. And again the messenger said gently 'Fear not, Mary!'

The star Lydia had seen in her first vision attracted her now to the hillside above the stable to which Mary and Joseph had been directed. There were mystified shepherds tumbling down the hillside towards the stable. They were babbling excitedly to each other. Why? What did they know? And by means of the cloth she was in front of that stable, the stable she would have at first refused for the Saviour of the world. The innkeeper's wife was fussing about usefully, in her element. Mary, exhausted and thankful, placed the swaddled child in a manger of hay as the shepherds stumbled in. The youngest of the three had brought a lamb with him and it settled happily in the straw, unperturbed by the larger beasts snorting and lowing without particular enthusiasm for the sight before them. But Lydia saw the child at ease with the beasts, the child spoken of in Isaiah, the child as perfect as God intended, before the disobedience of Adam and Eve. She saw that too in Mary, as the means for this wonderful birth. Here was the young Messiah revealed to the humble Jew in the persons of these simple shepherds. The good God throughout history has turned man's expectations upside down.

Lydia contemplated the sight with these thoughts, and her brow furrowed as she remembered her unanswered questions about kingship and about the manner of his redeeming power, nailed to a cross as he was, or would be.

By the star she was attracted again, and she saw three wealthy foreigners converge, their trains of camels and horses mingling as a braided plait. Each indicated that he had been guided from his distant land by the star. As she admired the beauty of their garments and riches carried in honour of Jesus, she was left with the glowing cloth in her hands, and Mary's question 'How shall this be?' ringing in her ears.

Lydia reasoned that these men from exotic lands had
been called to the child to show that, whatever the
nature of the kingship of the Messiah, he was
ordained to be the Messiah and Saviour of the whole
world for both Jew and Gentile. Chosen and
privileged were the Jews, the people of God, but they
clearly did not have sole custody of the Almighty
One as many seemed to believe. Perhaps all too were
to be subjects of the King. With this thought the cloth
then returned her to the hill of crucifixion, devoid of
bystanders. The cross looked majestic and
comforting. It was the sight upon which she could
not focus earlier, but now she could see once more
the inscription, to which had been added: 'and my
beloved Son in whom I am well pleased'. Beneath
was a golden crown in place of the evil thorns.
Jesus's face was free from pain, set in the attitude of
benevolent judgement. His body wore the cloth from
Lydia's hands, but transformed into a rich and
beautiful chasuble. A dove perched above his head,
and the rays from the cross embraced the bird in an
unburning fire. Lydia began to see that Jesus would
draw all mankind to himself as he reigned from the
cross. The nature of his kingship was fundamentally
at odds with her preconceptions, but the logic of it
was immediately apparent to her. However, she
knew that she was being prompted by this most
recent vision: something cataclysmic would have to
occur after his death on the cross. If she could find

out what that was, she would have the answer she desired.

Although life did not always seem to comprise the beautifully crafted hardwood components of an intricate wooden joint, her recent glimpses of the Divine profundities had convinced Lydia of the immaculate precision of God's Plan. There was nevertheless a piece missing – a dowel pin that would secure the whole. And in the adjacent room the message had been delivered to a bewildered Mary. 'Why should I be privy to all this?' Lydia asked, absently caressing the cloth, now over her left arm. Just as she began to suspect that the visions were tantalizingly at an end, the hoar-frost was about her and she was in the company of the foreign travellers outside the home of the innkeeper and his wife. A little way off, the stable housed only the beasts she had seen earlier: the manger was empty except for the hay.

She now saw inside the house: there was housed the Holy Family: Joseph, content, the watchful guardian; Mary with child in arms. What perfection! a foretaste of the Heavenly Realms where families will live continually in the presence of the Lord

Jesus. The principal travellers were shown to that family. They had persevered for months in their quest to understand the meaning of the bright star. They now gave the baby gifts signifying their understanding of his nature – and they were all correct. All contributed to the picture revealed to Lydia: gold for a king, incense for a God, and myrrh for a mortal. Jesus would be kingly, was the Son of God, but was taking human flesh. The cloth in Lydia's hands retained its aura of light, and she heard Mary's selfless acceptance of God's will: 'Let it be unto me according to your will'.

Lydia was fascinated by the sight of the empty manger and Jesus's translation to the home of the innkeeper. Was it of significance? She thought so.

— ❁ —

'Be it unto me according to your will.' Lydia again heard Mary's voice. Lydia's instruction was about to be concluded. She was fearful of doing anything that would cause her to lose contact with the visionary future. She buried her face in the cloth, and she saw the graveclothes discarded and folded in an empty sepulchre in the hillside. The large stone door had been thrust aside. Women were walking towards the tomb armed with myrrh and other burial spices intended for the anointment of the corpse: Mary led them. The scene merged with the placing of myrrh beside the infant in Bethlehem. And then Lydia found herself in a room with disciples she recognized from earlier visions; Mary also was there together with the woman whom Jesus had told to sin no more. And in the middle of them all appeared the King himself, risen from the dead, the scars of his crucifixion still visible.

'Peace be with you!' he said, and Lydia, privileged beyond measure, understood fleetingly the whole Divine Plan in place from the beginning of time. She saw the Holy Trinity of the Father, the Son and the Holy Spirit in the beauty of heaven and in the company of all saints – all those who had fulfilled their vocations in life, however modest the task or mean the duty. She saw that Jesus would indeed conquer death, and that his resurrection would swallow death absolutely; that nailed to the cross was all the sin of mankind; that mankind was now redeemable and redeemed, saved by the Son, for God the Father.

The detail of the visions soon faded like mist before the rays of the morning sun, leaving Lydia with a strong sense of faith and anticipation. She rose from her knees and took the cloth to Anne, folding it as she went, and from that moment the good news began to unfold over a hopeful and waiting mankind.

Appendix of Bible Readings

The Visions of the Shepherd

Genesis 1:26-28,31-2:2,2:15-17,3:6-19
Shepherd 1 – Isaiah 7:14,9:2,6-7
Shepherd 2 – Isaiah 40:1-5,9-11 and Malachi 3:2,4:2
Shepherd 3 – Luke 1:26-38
Shepherd 4 – Luke 1:39-55 and Matthew 1:20 (from: '... behold an angel ...')-23
Shepherd 5 – Luke 2:1-16
Shepherd 6 – Matthew 2:1-9
Shepherd 7 – Matthew 2:10-12
Shepherd 8 –
Shepherd 9 – John 1:1-14

The Visions of the Wise Men

Luke 1:26-38
Wise Men 1 – Luke 1:46-55
Wise Men 2 – Matthew 1:18-25
Wise Men 3 – Luke 2:1-20
Wise Men 4 – Matthew 2:1-10
Wise Men 5 – Luke 2:21-35
Wise Men 6 – Matthew 2:11-15
Wise Men 7 – Matthew 2:16-23
Wise Men 8 –
Wise Men 9 – John 1:1-14

The Visions of the Innkeeper

Isaiah 9:2,6-7
Innkeeper 1 – Micah 5:2-4
Innkeeper 2 – Isaiah 11:1-9
Innkeeper 3 – Isaiah 40:1-5,9-11 and Malachi 3:2,4:2
Innkeeper 4 – Luke 1:26-38
Innkeeper 5 – Matthew 1:18-23
Innkeeper 6 – Luke 2:8-16
Innkeeper 7 – Matthew 2:1-11
Innkeeper 8 –
Innkeeper 9 – John 1:1-14

The Visions of Herod the Great and the Servant-Girl

Isaiah 9:2,6-7
Herod 1 – Isaiah 11:1-9
Herod 2 – Micah 5:2-4
Herod 3 – Luke 1:26-38
Herod 4 – Matthew 1:18-23
Herod 5 – Luke 2:1-7
Herod 6 – Luke 2:8-16
Herod 7 – Matthew 2:1-11
Herod 8 –
Herod 9 – John 1:1-14

The Visions of the Centurion

Genesis 3:8-15
Centurion 1 – Genesis 22:15-18
Centurion 2 – Isaiah 9:2,6-7
Centurion 3 – Micah 5:2-4
Centurion 4 – Luke 1:26-38
Centurion 5 – Matthew 1:18-23

Centurion 6 – Luke 2:8-16
Centurion 7 – Matthew 2:1-11
Centurion 8 –
Centurion 9 – John 1:1-14

The Visions of Lydia

Genesis 3:8-15
Lydia 1 – Isaiah 9:2,6-7
Lydia 2 – Isaiah 11:1-9
Lydia 3 – Isaiah 60:1-6,19
Lydia 4 – Matthew 1:18-23
Lydia 5 – Luke 2:1-7
Lydia 6 – Luke 2:8-16
Lydia 7 – Matthew 2:1-11
Lydia 8 –
Lydia 9 – John 1:1-14

Notes

Notes

— ❀ —

....
....
....
....
....
....
....
....
....
....
....
....
....
....
....
....
....
....
....
....

Notes

— ❀ —

....
....
....
....
....
....
....
....
....
....
....
....
....
....
....
....
....
....
....

Notes

— ❀ —

Notes

....
....
....
....
....
....
....
....
....
....
....
....
....
....
....
....
....
....
....
....
....
....

Notes